Rapid Alphabet

Tablet ABCs

Written by G. Grafi
©2021

For my students.
Your eagerness to be
successful teachers has
created a need for this book.

Dear Parents and Teachers,

This alphabet book contains images intertwined within letters to aid in allowing students to associate letters and their corresponding sounds.

Each page follows a child with a tablet learning a different letter of the alphabet as the child observes a scene with more images whose first sounds correspond with those of the target letter.

Children are encouraged to review the letters and search for other words in the scenes that begin with the same sound.

This book is followed by a reading series that allows children to acquire reading skills from start to finish.

Dr. G. Grafi

Anna
AMBULANCE
a
Aa
Find other "a" words in the picture.
19:00 PM

Matt and Mel

Mm
Find other "m" words in the picture.
19:00 PM

Fara ❤ .
Ff
Find other "f" words in the picture.

Bob
Bb
Find other "b" words in the picture.
19:00 PM

Pam
Pp
POP!
POP!
Find other "p" words in the picture.
19:00 PM

Tom
Tt
t
Find other "t" words in the picture.
19:00 PM

Olga
Oo
Find other "o" words in the picture.
19:00 PM

Sam
Ss
Find other "s" words in the picture.
19:00 PM

Dino
Dd
Find other "d" words in the picture.
19:00 PM

Lara and Lana   .

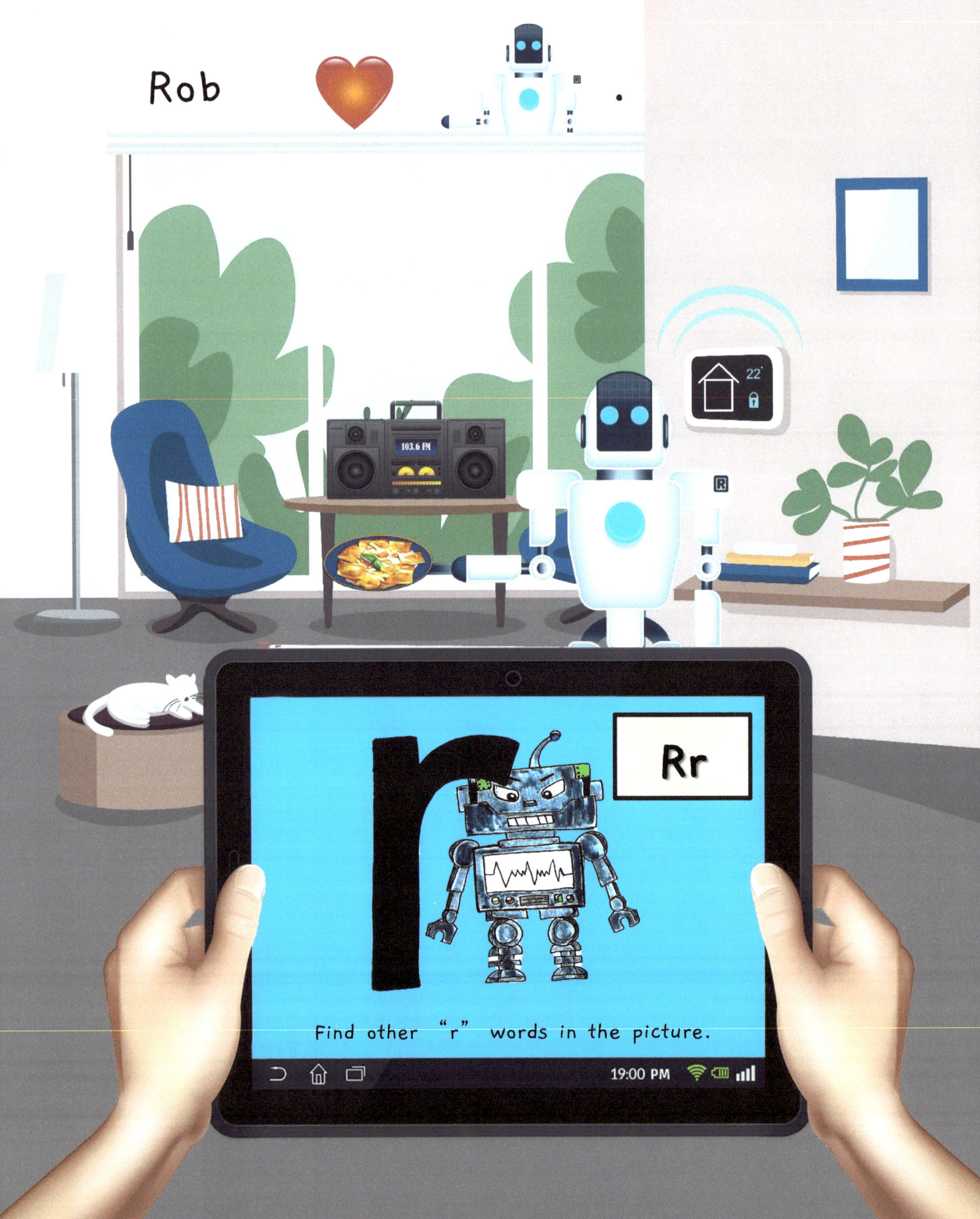
Rob
103.6 FM
r
Rr
Find other "r" words in the picture.
19:00 PM

Nat .

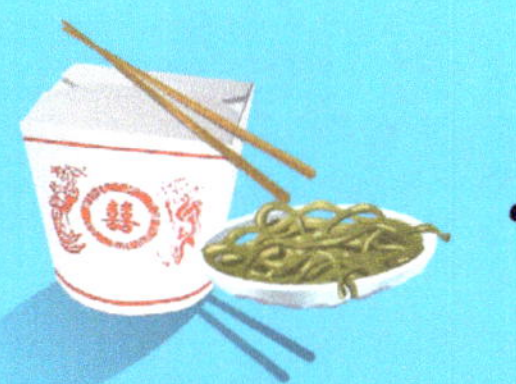

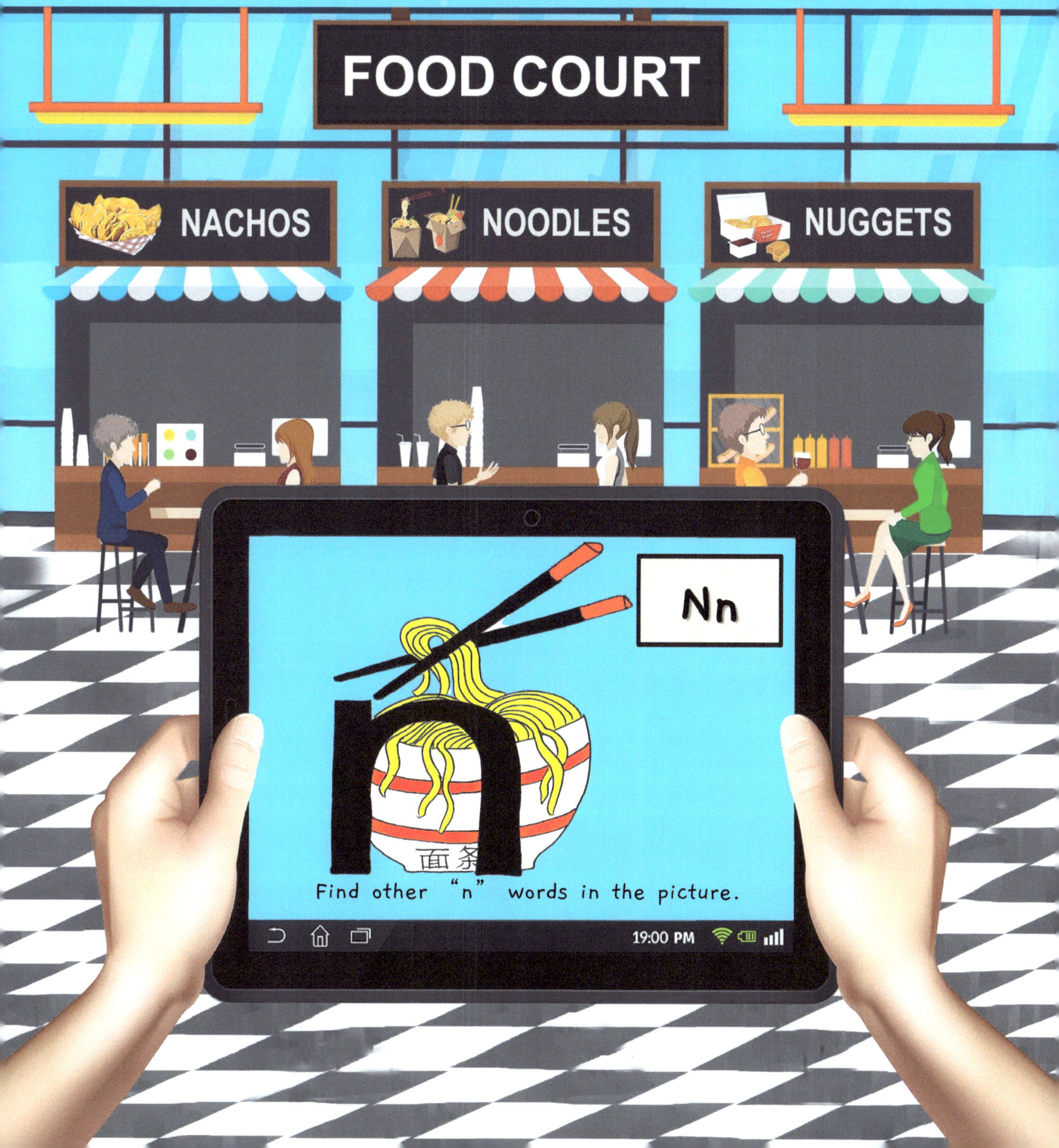
FOOD COURT
NACHOS
NOODLES
NUGGETS
Nn
面条
Find other "n" words in the picture.
19:00 PM

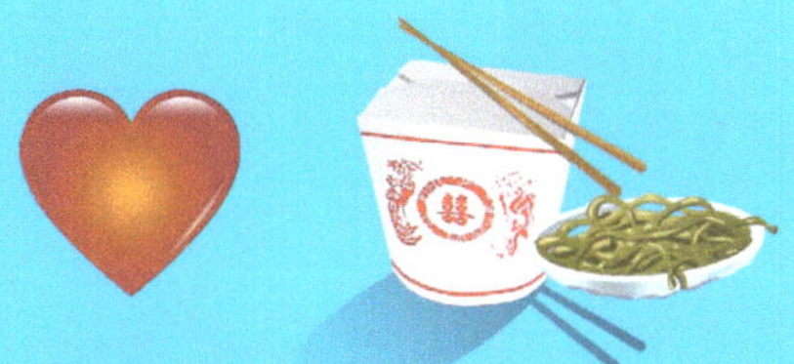

Inna
.
Ii
Find other "i" words in the picture.
19:00 PM

Gill
Gorilla Band
Globe Tour
Gg
Find other "g" words in the picture.
19:00 PM

Hana
Hh
Find other "h" words in the picture.
19:00 PM

Cam
Cc
Find other "c" words in the picture.
19:00 PM
Flakes

Will ❤ 🧇 .
Wow
Ww
Find other "w" words in the picture.
19:00 PM

Usher
Uu
Find other "u" words in the picture.
19:00 PM

Ed ❤️ 🌯.
Ee
Find other "e" words in the picture.
19:00 PM

Joe
JOKER
Jj
joker
Find other "j" words in the picture.
19:00 PM

Ken
Kk
Find other "k" words in the picture.
19:00 PM
Ketchup

Yara
Yy
Find other "y" words in the picture.
YOGURT
19:00 PM

Zara
Zig Zag
Zoo
October
Zombie Festival
Z
Zz
Find other "z" words in the picture.
19:00 PM

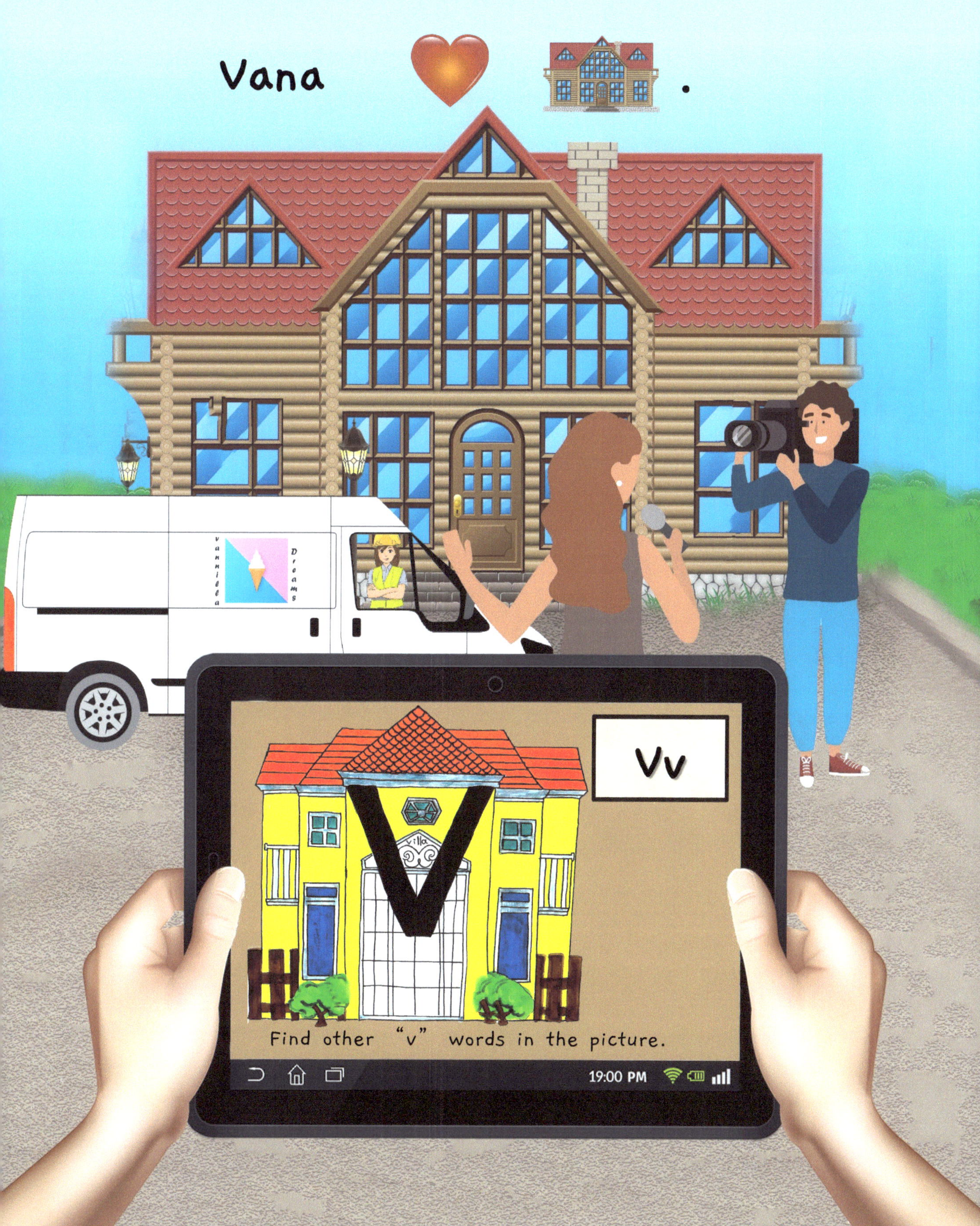

Vana
Vv
Find other "v" words in the picture.
vannilla Dreams
villa
19:00 PM

JaX ❤ X .
Today...
*Finish math- Find X
*Finish the teXt on your desks
* Who is X on the computer game?
2X = 2*X ?
X+3 = 5
FIND X...
12
9
3
6
Xx
Find other "x" words in the picture.
19:00 PM

Quin
Quiet
Quack Quack
Qu
qu
Find other "qu" words in the picture.
quack quack!
19:00 PM